{99}Ways
to Entertain Your
Family for Free

99 Ways
to Entertain Your
Family for Free

Mack Thomas

WaterBrook
PRESS

99 WAYS TO ENTERTAIN YOUR FAMILY FOR FREE
Published by WaterBrook Press
12265 Oracle Boulevard, Suite 200
Colorado Springs, Colorado 80921

ISBN 978-0-307-45836-0
ISBN 978-0-307-45842-1 (electronic)

Published in the United States by WaterBrook Multnomah, an imprint of the Crown Publishing Group, a division of Random House Inc., New York.

WATERBROOK and its deer colophon are registered trademarks of Random House Inc.

Library of Congress Cataloging-in-Publication Data
Thomas, Mack.
    99 ways to entertain your family for free! / Mack Thomas. — 1st ed.
        p. cm.
    ISBN: 978-0-307-45836-0 — ISBN 978-0-307-45842-1 (electronic)
1. Family recreation—United States. I. Title. II. Title: Ninety-nine ways to entertain your family for free!
    GV182.8.T48 2009
    790.1'.91—dc22

                    2009013391

Printed in the United States of America
2009—First Edition

10 9 87 6 5 4 3 2 1

SPECIAL SALES
Most WaterBrook Multnomah books are available at special quantity discounts when purchased in bulk by corporations, organizations, and special-interest groups. Custom imprinting or excerpting can also be done to fit special needs. For information, please e-mail SpecialMarkets@WaterBrookMultnomah.com or call 1-800-603-7051.

Contents

Introduction

This book is really about more than getting the best deal on entertainment. Even if we could afford the most lavishly expensive diversions available, they're less valuable—and ultimately less satisfying—than the kinds of entertainment promoted in this book. So not only will you be getting something here for free...you'll be getting the *best* for free.

In fact, the qualities, attitudes, mindsets, and skills that let us enjoy to the max *any* kind of entertainment are best learned in the kinds of activities you'll be guided through in this book.

So, at root, this is more about learning to enjoy better all of life than about being entertained more economically. Though the dollar savings are no small matter. Based on a conservative average expenditure of $7.50 per person for a paid entertainment event, this book will save a family of four about $3,000 annually.

If You're Bored, You're Boring
The foundational concept here is probably this: truly satisfying entertainment comes from an *active* attitude and approach, not

passive. It's about taking the lead to engage in what's happening all around us, knowing there'll always be something interesting and delightful about it.

In other words, you're only as bored as you choose to be.

As our five children were growing up, my wife and I tried to teach them that if a person is bored, it's because he himself is boring. It means he's self-focused (instead of looking outward with attentiveness and a readiness to interact). Who could be more boring than someone sitting there, demanding to be entertained? It's as if that person is chained in the prison of self.

So you may want to strike from your family's vocabulary the phrase "I'm bored." Replace it with an attitude that affirms, "There's something enjoyable and interesting here, and *I'm going to find it.*" Build that into your family…and you'll all be not only happier and more satisfied but also more free.

You'll also be more ready for life's realities that go beyond entertainment. Half a century ago, in a letter written to a mother, C. S. Lewis quoted eighteenth-century British author Samuel Johnson: "To be happy at home is the end of all human endeavor." One reason to seek such happiness, Lewis said, is "to prepare for being happy in our own real home hereafter."

May this book help increase the kind of happiness in your family that indeed nudges all of you toward heave and its lasting joys.

1 Indoors

Live in harmony with one another.

—ROMANS 12:16

Here's step number one for the best indoor entertainment: escape and unplug from electronic media as much as possible. When it comes to entertainment, you have better things to do—more enriching and healthier, more restorative and recreational—with your time and your brain cells.

Yes, there's a valid place in our lives for electronic technology, but life's too short to give it the amount of time that it tends to addictively suck from us. Plus, electronic media often tend to separate families more than unite them. After all, you're not primarily a collection of screen-frozen, lock-eyed, keypad-punching individuals; you're a *family.*

Get in the habit of doing things that regularly get you talking together, thinking together, sharing together, laughing together—and enjoying the new sparkle in one another's eyes.

1   Never Bored with Board Games

On a stay-inside, disagreeable-weather day, have a board game marathon. Have everyone choose a favorite board game, and take turns playing them all.

For some variety, allow the person who chose the game to make one rule change in how that game is played, and make it a fun alteration. For example, in Scrabble, give everyone a five- or ten-point bonus score for each word they play that includes a letter in their name. Or in Monopoly, charge everyone a fifty-dollar fee, payable to the bank, each time they complete their turn without saying either "please" or "thank you." Or in Clue, have *two* murderers responsible for the crime (sharing the same weapon) instead of just one. In Risk, divide the players into two alliances who strategize together and never attack each other; one alliance wins whenever just one person on the opposing side has all her troops eliminated.

2   Picture This

Get out your old family photos and go through them together. You may want to sort and organize them as you go, but the main point is simply to enjoy them together. Take plenty of time to reminisce.

Together choose your top three, five, or ten photos in several categories; for example, funniest, weirdest, coolest, most embarrassing, most revealing, happiest occasion, most serious occasion, most tired occasion, most energetic occasion, most awkward occasion, most formal occasion, most relaxed occasion, best shot for a family Christmas card, best shot for a family scrapbook cover, best shot for a "wanted" poster, and best shot for a national magazine cover (just in case you get asked!).

Also identify your oldest family photo (perhaps one of grandparents or great-grandparents).

Make a visual family tree, with a favorite photo of each person.

3 FAMILY CREST

To best illustrate and symbolize each person's personality in your family, have them each choose a living creature (lion, eagle, ox, gazelle, tiger, spider, dragonfly, etc.) or plant (sagebrush, daisy, heather, rose, oak tree, lily, wheat stalk, pine tree, apple tree, etc.) or some other object (lighthouse, book, rock, hammer, shield, nest, etc.). In the same way, choose symbols in these categories that best represent your family as a whole. (Also research the meaning of your family name, and think about how to indicate it visually and symbolically.)

At the library or online, research the topic of heraldry. Design your own family crest or coat of arms, or individual crests, that will incorporate the symbols you've chosen.

You can illustrate all this on posters. Or make a family banner (or banners for each person) using cloth fragments and old sheets and towels, etc.

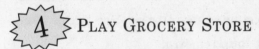 PLAY GROCERY STORE

Is it time to reorganize the pantry or kitchen cabinet shelves? Take out everything and let the kids play grocery store with the unopened items. Load their "merchandise" onto their toy wagon, which they can pull into the playroom or out to the garage or back patio. (Help them out by carrying a few box loads or bag loads.)

Give them blank stickers or sticky notes and a marker to indicate prices and sale items. Also supply them with your used grocery bags.

For money, use pennies and nickels from a piggy bank, or something you have lots of, like beans or uncooked macaroni. A pocket calculator can serve as the cash register, and a shoebox can be a cash drawer. (Let them use a money box, if you have one.)

In the same way, they can play clothing store (when you re-organize your closets) and hardware store (when you clean out the garage).

5 — SHOW TIME

Playact Bible stories, nursery rhymes, fairy tales, and adventure stories. The best choices are whatever the kids have recently read themselves or listened to and enjoyed.

Improvise a stage. A corner of the room with the furniture moved back will work fine. If you want a curtain, string a line and hang a bedsheet.

A few simple items—a box or crate, a chair, a pillow, a towel—can be all-purpose props. The finest backdrops are imaginary, but you can also craft one by painting or drawing on poster paper or an old bedsheet. Improvise your costumes as well, focusing especially on color.

Practice the scenes. But the point is just to have fun, not perfection. Does it turn out differently every time you go through it? That's great! The more you're simply enjoying it yourselves, the more enjoyable it will be for others to watch.

So invite an audience—grandparents, neighbors, friends.

6 SHUFFLE AND DEAL

This entire book could be filled to overflowing with descriptions of fun card games for your kids. It's astonishing how much you can do with a simple deck of cards.

From your own childhood, you probably remember go fish, slapjack, old maid, war, and concentration (memory). Later you may have learned crazy eights, hearts, spades, rummy, pinochle, canasta, poker, or others (there are literally hundreds of recognized games, counting all the variations). If you've forgotten the rules to your favorites, dig out your copy of *Hoyle's Rules of Games* (or check online—several Internet sites offer card game rules), and teach the rest of the family as you refresh yourself.

Learn as many games as possible, constantly adding new ones to your family's repertoire.

You can play at the kitchen or dining-room table, seated on the floor around a coffee table, or sprawled on a rug by the fireplace.

7 TENT TIME

Use chair cushions, blankets, and beach towels to make tents in the living room. To provide more hanging support, stretch cords or ropes tied to sturdy furniture, door knobs, etc. Dining-room chairs can also offer good support.

Eat lunch among the tents, dinner too. (Hot dogs are great for the occasion.) Bring stuffed animals and favorite toys inside the tents—play cards and board games too.

Pull in sleeping bags and spend the night there. Use only flashlights for light. Then use the flashlights and your hands to make shadow forms on the tent walls.

In the dark, swap ghost stories, hero stories, funny stories. Tell jokes, sing camp songs, make weird noises. (Who can make the loudest snore?) And see who can stay silent the longest.

When morning comes, have pancakes or waffles for breakfast.

8 THE BIG BUILDUP

Let your kids bring all their building-block toys (like Legos) to a place where they don't usually play with them—the dining-room table, the garage floor, the back patio. In this special location on this special day, let everyone work together to build something different than they ever have—and if possible, bigger than ever.

Construct a massive city with skyscrapers. Or a sports stadium. Or a mountain fortress. Or a space station. Or a military base. Or a motion-picture studio. At the start of the day, decide and design together (roughly at least) what you want to make, then go for it. Meanwhile, be flexible enough for plenty of redesigns along the way.

Incorporate whatever additional building materials you can scrape together. Make your own landscape accessories with paper, cardboard, and colored markers.

9 ⟩ THE FAMILY GALLERY

Take a week to focus together on creative visual arts. Display the results prominently throughout your home, and invite friends and relatives over on a special evening to enjoy your creations.

Using whatever you have on hand, explore every medium that may hold interest for anyone in your family. Create pictures with finger paints, crayons, pastels, watercolors, colored markers, pens, and pencils.

Cut out colored paper strips (or pictures from magazines) and glue them together to form a collage or montage. Be creative— use newspaper clippings, junk mail, movie-ticket stubs, product packaging—whatever you can find and put together in a creative way.

Apply glue to sheets of paper and make patterns of rice, lentils, beans, peas, dried macaroni, etc.

Create sculptures using homemade molding clay or fragments of wood, metal, plastic, and other materials from anything that's been lying around unused.

10 YOUR HOLLYWOOD DEBUT

Put on one of your family's favorite movies, one you've all seen many times. Turn off the sound and supply the dialogue as much as you can from memory. If you can't remember lines, make them up, perhaps altering the content and emotional tone of the scenes as you see fit. Allow the characters to say what you suppose they're *really* thinking.

Do the same thing with some movie you've never seen— perhaps a low-budget or cheesy movie you wouldn't normally watch. Make the producers wish they'd used *you* as the screenwriter!

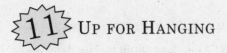 **11** Up for Hanging

Play the hangman game. One person draws a hangman's post (like a big upside-down L). He then thinks of a random word and draws underlines for however many letters it has (_ _ _ _ _ for *funky*).

One person starts guessing which letters are used in the word, selecting one alphabet letter at a time. Correct letter guesses are marked down in the blank underlines. (A letter used multiple times needs to be guessed only once, and all occurrences are filled in.)

For every *in*correct guess, the first player adds a body part to dangle from the hangman's post—head, then torso, then the two arms separately, and finally the two legs separately. If all six parts are added before the word is guessed and all the letters are filled in, that player loses, and the hangman wins.

12 Make Your Mark

More pencil-and-paper games:

Five Lines: One person thinks of something to draw and starts her illustration with five correctly placed but unconnected lines (straight or curved). The next player decides what those five lines most likely represent, then he adds five more lines reflecting his perception of it. They keep exchanging the paper and adding five lines each turn, always continuing with their own original concept in mind. They keep going until someone sees enough to figure out what the other's trying to draw.

Connect the Dots: Make a square grid of aligned dots, with about a dozen dots in each rank and file. The players take turns drawing one line from dot to dot (one line per turn). If a player's line completes a square, she puts her initial in that square. The winner is the one with the most initialed boxes.

13 > SUPER TICK-TACK-TOE

Draw nine tick-tack-toe games (each with nine squares) all stacked together to form one giant supersquare that is three games high and three games wide. Mark heavier lines around each game area, and use lighter lines for the smaller squares inside each game. (It's very important to see each game separately while you play.)

Now here's the trick: each player's choice of square determines the game in which the next player must play.

For example: Bethany goes first and decides to mark her first

X inside the upper-left square of one of the game areas. The next player, Sam, must then mark his O on any square in the upper-left game. Within that upper-left game, let's say Sam puts his O in the middle square. On her next turn Bethany must then place her X on any square in the middle game. And so on.

Each player must keep following the other's lead like this, unless the game where they would normally mark next is already filled with Xs and Os. The winner is the one who has the most three-in-a-rows.

14 ⟩ BOARD GAME CRAZINESS

Mix it up. In Chinese checkers, let each person complete one turn, then rotate the board one star point to the left so that each person now is playing with the colored pieces played earlier by the person on her right. After everyone has played one more turn like this, rotate again, and keep doing so each round. The winner will be whoever is first to fill the opposite star point with whatever color he happens to be playing with on that particular turn.

While two of you are playing regular checkers, have someone else nearby operating a timer or stopwatch at different time intervals. (You can also use an egg timer.) Each time the interval ends, the two players have to rotate the board and play the opposing side. The winner is still whoever jumps and captures the other player's last checker—but neither one knows yet what color she'll be playing when that time comes.

15 Costume Department

Spend creative hours together assembling lots of costumes for your own handy supply—like the costume department in a movie studio. These will be put to good use in playtime as well as in skits and drama sketches you'll want to do as a family.

Use old clothes, cloth scraps, or other fabric (such as old curtains, towels, etc.—even rugs). Make basic throw-over tunics that can be adapted in a variety of ways. Also fashion the more detailed costumes of the characters and eras you're most interested in (frontier days, the Middle Ages, Bible times, etc.). Use scissors to cut and piece the garments, and hold them together with safety pins or fabric tape.

If you need more raw material, sometimes a thrift store will have a freebies table with clothing items. If so, take all you can.

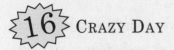

16 CRAZY DAY

Make a day where everything's backward or confused or out of whack.

Wear your clothes inside out, mismatched in color and style, or in the totally wrong season (shorts and T-shirts in December, or earmuffs in June).

Do something weird in every room. Turn lampshades upside down, fling all the kitchen cabinet doors open wide, and place a bouquet of flowers in the toilet bowl. Make the beds with the pillows at the foot. Toss the throw rugs on the lawn instead of the family-room floor. Turn tables and stools upside down. Hang socks or underwear on the dining-room chandelier. Put the toaster in the refrigerator. On bookshelves, turn the books so all their spines face inward. Put the toothpaste tube on the kitchen stovetop, the salt and pepper shakers on the fireplace mantle, and the magazine rack in the bathtub.

17 FAMILY IN MOTION

It's time to dance! Put on your favorite music and glide, rock, shake, boogie, hop, swing, strut, twist, leap, and whirl. Put on different styles of music and improvise your movements. If you have ethnic tunes, try the hula, an Irish jig, Russian squat kicks, or a Chinese dragon dance.

If you know some traditional or folk dances, teach everyone all the steps you know. Likewise with square dance and ballroom steps.

Tape quarters or half dollars to the soles of your shoes and tap-dance.

Form a single file, with everyone holding the waist of the person in front, and dance a conga line through the whole house.

Create your own family dance with definite sequences and movements, all choreographed to your favorite song. Practice so everyone can do it together (without making all this a burden or a chore).

18 INDOOR TREASURE

Set up an indoor treasure hunt where many of the clues are decoded from the words found in the family's books.

For example, give the hunters a paper-strip clue with this information: "*DBWS* by Stewart Edward White. 38-136. 139-265. 217-87." That means they'll look on the family-room bookshelf for a volume by Stewart Edward White with a title whose initials are DBWS. (It's the classic biography *Daniel Boone: Wilderness Scout.*) Explain the number coding: each is a page number followed by a word number.

When they find White's book, they'll discover that "yellow" is the 136th word on page 38, "pack" is the 265th word on page 139, and "within" is the 87th word on page 217. Putting all that together (*yellow, pack, within*), they'll run to find a yellow back-pack and look inside. Sure enough, your next clue for them will be there.

⟨19⟩ MAGAZINE SCAVENGE

Before you toss that stack of old magazines, have a scavenger hunt among their pages.

Place the magazines on the floor in the middle of the room, and give everyone a list of things to look for in the magazines' pictures. Locate them and tear or cut them out. Find as many of each kind of picture as you can. Afterward, look at everyone's collections and choose together the most creative and interesting finds in each category.

A few examples of what to look for would be someone wearing a helmet, someone wearing sunglasses, a closed door, an open window, something orange, something both black and white, something with at least six different colors, something normally cold, something normally hot, red wheels, something four-legged, something thin and flat, something soaked, something broken, something spotted, something wrinkled, money, an ocean view, something that flies, something that crawls.

20 PAPER NIGHT

Have an activity night when everything's done with paper—making paper-bag masks, paper-bag puppets, paper airplanes, paper rockets, paper boats, paper birds, paper fish, paper dolls, paper castles, paper kites, paper fans, paper necklaces, paper hats, paper flowers, paper stars, paper snowflakes, paper collages, paper cubes, paper cylinders, paper pyramids...paper *anything*. Be creative!

Use any kinds of paper you have on hand. Also bring out scissors, tape, a stapler, and crayons or colored markers.

If you know origami-folding methods, teach them to the entire family. (The basic folds are featured online at several Web sites, as are the instructions for elaborate paper airplanes and boats and other paper toys.)

And just for the occasion, temporarily paper one of the family-room walls with old Sunday comics. Serve dinner on paper plates and cups.

21 RING ON A STRING

Here's a fun deception game. Everyone sits in a circle (on the floor or in chairs) except for one person who's It and stands inside the circle. The others hold both their fists loosely around a cord or string that wraps its way around the entire circle (with the ends tied together). On the cord is a ring or similar small object that can be easily glided along and slipped from one person to the next—while mostly kept hidden beneath their fists. The ring *must* keep moving.

As the ring is being continually passed, everyone around the circle keeps sliding her fists back and forth along the cord, whether she has the ring or not.

The object of the game is for the person who's It to correctly identify who's got the ring at any time. That person then becomes It.

22 SHOW AND TELL—IF YOU CAN

Play telephone Pictionary. Each person has a blank sheet of paper. At the top, they write an interesting one-line sentence (such as the opening to a story). Then everyone passes their sheet to the left.

Each person reads silently the sentence on the page that was passed to them. Just below it, they try to illustrate what it says. Then they fold over the top of the page so only their drawing is showing (the sentence is hidden). Again, everyone passes their sheet to the left.

Now each person writes a sentence that matches the illustration they see. They fold the paper again to hide the drawing (only the new sentence is showing) and again pass it to the left.

This process keeps going until everyone has done something on each page. Then unfold them and read them all aloud. You'll be amazed at the hilarious misinterpretations!

23 ☆ TAP-CLAP-SNAP

Everyone sits in a circle and numbers off, 1, 2, 3, etc.

Then in unison, follow repeatedly this steady six-beat sequence: tap your knees twice with your palms, clap hands twice, snap left finger, snap right finger. Everyone maintains a steady tempo while repeatedly cycling through this sequence. (You can all speed it up later.)

Player No. 1 begins the competition. With her left-finger snap, she calls out her own number ("One"), then with her right-finger snap, she simultaneously calls another player's number ("Five," for example).

On the next left-finger snap, player No. 5 now calls out his number, and on the right-finger snap, he calls out someone else's number, who then calls the numbers the next time, and so on. You're eliminated whenever you say the wrong number or respond too late. The winner is the person still in after all the others are out.

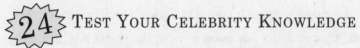 24 TEST YOUR CELEBRITY KNOWLEDGE

Play guess the celebrity. Each person writes down the names of at least ten famous people (contemporary or historic) whose names are well known by your family. Also include (a) fictional characters from books, movies, mythology, etc.; (b) other recognizable personifications like the man in the moon or Mother Nature; and (c) friends, relatives, and neighbors you all know by name.

Cut or tear your list so each name is on a separate strip of paper. Fold the strips once, then toss them into a hat or basket.

Divide into teams. Use a timer to limit each team's turn. During their turn, one player on each team pulls out names and gives clues to help his teammates guess the name. Each player gets one free pass per turn if he pulls out a name he doesn't know. Keep score.

25 YES OR NO?

Play twenty questions. One person thinks of a specific object, without revealing to the others what it is. The others take turns asking questions that must be answered either yes or no. (Examples: "Is it in this room?" "Does it belong to you?" "Will it fit in a suitcase?" "Have I ever used it?")

During a turn, each person is allowed to ask only one question. That includes any guess of what the object is. ("Is it that candlestick on the mantle?")

The first person answers each question honestly. Whoever correctly guesses the object is the winner and gets to choose the next object for everyone else to guess in the next round. If no one guesses it correctly after twenty questions have been asked, the first person gets to go again, using a different object.

26 LOTS OF FUN FOR LITTLE ONES

Let these suggestions stimulate even more of your ideas:

- Play tumbling tower. Build it out of empty, round salt-boxes and oatmeal boxes, or shoeboxes, or any other cardboard boxes. Then knock the tower down. Do it all over again.

- Play school. Play church. Play store. Play office. Play zoo. Play circus.

- Sail boats in the bathtub. Create storms and waves. Or pretend you're fishing.

- Dress up your pets in play clothes.

- Paint with pudding. Make chocolate pudding, then on a washable surface (like a countertop) finger-paint with it.

- Dress up in bedsheets and pretend you're ghosts.

- Pretend your bed is a stagecoach, a big semitrailer truck, or a bus—and take a long adventurous trip somewhere.

- Tape blank white paper on windows where the sun shines through, and then draw and color on the pages.

27 ⟩ MORE INDOOR FUN

Try these activities:

- Play the hot and cold game. Choose an object together, then one of you hides it somewhere after everyone else steps out of the room. As the others come back in to search for it, give clues about how close anyone's getting—by saying "cold," "cool," "warm," "warmer," "hot," "very hot," etc. But don't indicate which one of them is closest; let them figure that out for themselves while they hunt.

- Play what's under the blanket? While the others are out of the room, place an object on the floor and spread a blanket on top of it. The others have to guess what it is by looking at the shape.

- Have a chess tournament. Teach everyone the rules.

- Have each person create her own crossword puzzle—from simple to complex. Pass them around and take turns solving them.

 ## 28 STILL MORE INDOOR FUN

- Learn how to juggle. Practice together.

- Are some of you collectors? Spread out your collections some night for everyone to see. Turn the family room into a museum.

- Have a trade day where everyone in the family wears one another's clothes and shoes and sits at that person's place at the dinner table.

- Act out the stories of the books you've been reading together and enjoying. A good one to start with is *The*

Lion, the Witch and the Wardrobe from C. S. Lewis's Chronicles of Narnia.

- Pull out an old jigsaw puzzle from the closet, spread out the pieces on the dining-room table, and let everyone work on putting it together.
- Pretend for one night that you're living in the days before electricity. Do everything by candlelight or the light of an oil lamp.

SUMMARY

In this section you've seen twenty-eight ways (and more) of entertaining your family for free inside your home. No need to go far to have fun. Try out as many as you can, and as you find a few that work best for your family, return to them again and again, refining them to make them your very own tradition.

2 Outdoors

Encourage each other and give each other strength.

—1 THESSALONIANS 5:11

In general, if the choice is between doing something inside or outside—run straight out the back door.

Being outside almost always means more exercise and energy expenditure, not to mention soaking up healthy sunshine and fresh air. A big rash of alarming statistics about today's families—like those regarding obesity, mental myopia, and more—would dramatically improve if families simply spent more time being active outdoors.

Hopefully, being out there will also mean being more outgoing in relationships with neighbors. Many of these activities will have their fun quotient greatly multiplied simply by having more folks involved. So invite them over, though they might be dropping by anyway when they hear the fun shouts and laughter resounding from your backyard.

29 ⟩ New Construction

If there's a home construction site or remodeling site nearby, and you see unwanted construction material scraps discarded outside (especially lumber and plyboard), ask for permission to take enough of the scraps to build a makeshift clubhouse in your backyard. It won't necessarily be anything long-lasting—just fun.

Use whatever leftover nails you can find to nail it all together. You can add to it with cardboard pieces, affixed with tape, staples, or tacks. Give the whole thing a lavish coat of paint from any old cans in the garage (the more colors the better). Add anything else you have available—carpet scraps, old window screens, unused shelving, bricks and cinder blocks, leftover vinyl or tile flooring. (*Now* you know why you've saved that stuff all this time!)

Name this new place, and put a sign over the door.

30 ⟩ Family Olympics

Gather in the backyard (with friends and neighbors) for athletic competition, with medals (colored cardboard cutouts hanging from ribbons) for the winners.

Try events like these: somersaults; cartwheels; rolling all the way across the lawn without touching your hands or feet to the ground; hopping across the lawn one-legged; walking a long, thin plank (or broomstick) without stepping off; crab-walk racing; handstands; standing long jump; obstacle course made of old tires to step in and over; hurdling over lawn furniture; tossing a tennis ball (or other object) into a bucket from ever-increasing distances; balancing a baseball bat on its end; racing with an egg (or olive or Ping-Pong ball) on a spoon held by the handle in your teeth; water-balloon toss; pea-shooting through soda straws; broom toss (for distance); and whatever else you can think of.

 ## HAVING FUN WHILE GETTING FIT

These games provide great exercise as well as fun:

- *Three-legged race:* The racing partners each have one leg bound to the other.

- *Arm wrestling:* To avoid injury, remember to pivot your shoulder so you're always facing toward your wrestling hand as it goes down.

- *Jumping rope:* Try it one-legged, alternating your feet, and also crisscross your hands.

- *Wheelbarrow race:* One player walks on his hands while his ankles are held by his partner—the driver.

- *Sack race:* Pull a gunnysack or pillowcase over your feet and legs and go for it.
- *Leg wrestling:* Two players lie side by side on their backs, in different directions, each with an arm linked to the other person's. At the signal, they raise their inside leg three times. On the third count, they hook each other's upraised leg and try to pull over their opponent.

32 ANNIE OVER

Split into two even teams—one in the front yard with a tennis ball or rubber playground ball, and the other around back. The first team yells out, "Annie!" After hearing the backyard team respond by yelling, "Over," the first team throws the ball over the roof so it rolls down the other side to be caught by someone in back.

The second team's goal is to run and tag the other team's players with the ball before they safely reach the backyard without getting tagged. (The fun is in never knowing from which direction the other players will come around the house.) Any player tagged by the ball must join the opposing team.

The next round starts with each team on the opposite side of the house from where it started. The game continues until everyone ends up on one team.

33 ⬡ Bag It

Try these activities, each one using a bag:

- *Bag kites:* On a windy day, make kites with plastic grocery bags. They really catch the wind.
- *Fast trash contest:* Give everyone a trash bag, go to a playground, to a park, or along a neighborhood street, and pick up litter. The person filling her bag first is the winner.
- *Bag skits:* This is a good one to do with neighbors. Fill a couple of paper bags with several unrelated objects— some of them commonplace, others rather odd. Gather everyone on the back patio and divide into teams. Each team gets a bag, and they must prepare a skit using all the items inside it as props. Let each team go away on their own a few minutes to put together their production. Then enjoy each other's dramatics!

34 ⬡ Biking Time

Ride your bikes together and make the most of it.

On a bike trail or other safe route, ride single file and play follow the leader. This goes especially well when there are criss-crossing trails, turnouts, loops, and lots of other options.

The leader can alternate between riding superslow or su-perfast (as long as everyone can keep up). Pedal with only the left foot, then only the right. Ride standing or seated.

In a large empty parking lot or any other rideable open space, the leader can make a big figure eight, or even a double or triple figure eight. Then make it just the right size—and go just the right speed—so you alternate passing each other where the loops join.

If you can set up some ramps or other obstacles, those can enhance the fun.

35 FIVE HUNDRED BALL

Use a football, baseball, or softball for this game. For younger players, use a rubber playground ball.

One person is the thrower, and all the others catch.

Before each throw, the thrower yells out a number divisible by fifty. The person who catches the ball earns that many points on that particular throw. If a person touches the ball but doesn't catch it before it touches the ground, the points are deducted from his score.

The first person to reach five hundred points then becomes the thrower.

If the thrower yells "Double" before the throw, the successful catcher doubles his previous point total; but if someone touches the ball without catching it, his previous point total is cut in half.

If the thrower yells "Jackpot," the successful catcher automatically becomes the next thrower; but if someone touches the ball without catching it, his previous point total goes back to zero.

36 GOOD DEEDS ANONYMOUS

Have fun working together to serve someone in an unexpected way. Make a game of it. See if you can pull off your good deed without being discovered.

After an overnight snowfall, get up early and go together to a friend's or neighbor's house to silently shovel the driveway and sidewalk. Then come back home and enjoy your favorite hot breakfast. Or go late at night (moonlight will help you to see) and rake up someone's fallen leaves. Or when you know a neighbor's away on vacation, mow her lawn before she returns.

To serve a larger group, go to a public rest room and give it a thorough cleaning. See how fast you can get inside, get it done, and get out. Or clean up the trash in a park or along a neighborhood street or highway.

 HOME FREE

Try variations of hide-and-seek, like these:

Sardines: Only the person who's It hides; everyone else counts together to a hundred (or whatever), then they all spread out to seek the hiding one. As each person finds him, they join him in his hiding spot. The last person to find the spot where all the others are packed in is the new It.

Kick the can: Works like normal hide-and-seek, except those who are caught and tagged by whoever's It have to go inside a marked-off "jail" and stay there. Nearby, out in the open, is an empty can. Any player who isn't caught yet can free everyone who's in jail by rushing up and kicking the can (while avoiding being tagged by It). But if everyone winds up in jail, the person who's been in jail the longest is the new It.

38 PLAY FOUR SQUARE

In a flat area, mark off a square measuring sixteen to twenty feet across. Divide it into equal quadrants, numbered one to four. One person stands in each quadrant.

The player in the fourth quadrant has a rubber playground ball and begins play by bouncing it into the lowest-numbered quadrant. Using only his hands, the player there then bounces it into any other quadrant, and so on. Play continues until someone is eliminated by (a) letting the ball bounce more than once in her square; (b) failing to hit it into another square; (c) hitting it out of bounds; (d) holding or carrying the ball, or (e) touching it with any part of her body except the hands.

The person eliminated steps off; the others below her each move to a higher-numbered square, and a new player joins in the first square.

39 RAINY DAY RELEASE

When it's raining, go out and make the most of it. Find the best splash puddles, and splash them dry. Fill your rain boots with water. Turn your umbrellas upside down.

In soggy mud holes, build tiny dams and water channels

and lakes. Make mud cakes, mud pies, mud steaks, and mud bread.

On a slope, slide on the slippery wet grass.

Play soccer or football in the rain. Play basketball and pound puddles as you dribble. Or ride your bikes through puddles and watch the water fling out from your speeding wheels.

Stand under rain-soaked trees, grab the lower branches, give them a hearty shake, and drench yourself even more.

Stand under the river that's flowing out from a gutter spout on a roof.

Sing in the rain.

40 RED ROVER

Invite other families and friends to join you in this game—and since this may get a little physical, don't play with younger children and caution everyone not to run too fast and hard! Divide into two equal teams. Each team stands in a line, with arms outstretched and hands tightly clasped. The two lines face each other, several yards apart.

The teams take turns calling out the name of a person on the other team. The designated person runs and tries to break through a hand link at some point in the other team's line.

To summon the person (Shawna, for example) from the other team, the first team yells out in unison, "Red rover, red rover, send *Shawna* right over!" Then Shawna takes off running. If she doesn't break the link, she must join the other team. But if she's successful in breaking through, Shawna chooses someone to take back with her to join her own team.

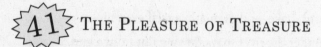 ## 41 ⟩ THE PLEASURE OF TREASURE

Set up a wide-ranging outdoor treasure hunt. The treasure can be candy or snacks you have on hand or some other gift you've been saving. Find a good hiding place for the treasure that no one will suspect.

Write a series of clues, with each clue leading to the spot where the next clue can be found. The last clue will lead straight to the treasure.

Don't make the clues too obvious. Force everyone to really think.

For extra fun, use both sides of the paper strips on which the clues are found. One side gives complete instructions where to find the next clue. The other is part of a puzzle—you need all the strips joined together to figure out the final clue of where the treasure is.

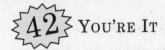

42 YOU'RE IT

Try new and different rules each time you play tag. Variations are endless. Here are just a few:

- *Freeze tag:* After getting tagged by whoever's It, you have to stand still—frozen—until another player tags you to immediately thaw you.

- *Tunnel tag:* After getting tagged, you stay where you are and spread your legs wide apart. To release you, another player has to pass between your legs.

- *Spud* (one of the best): At the start, everyone clusters together. Whoever's It throws a ball high in the air, and everyone else starts running outward. When It catches the ball, he yells "Spud!" and everyone else has to stop and stand still. Then It takes three steps in any direction and throws the ball at another player (she can dodge the throw, but her feet must stay planted.) If he's hit, he's It.

Try creating your own new rules as well.

43 ONLY IN AUTUMN

Before raking up fallen leaves, make big piles to romp in, kick around, and splash through. Bury yourselves in them. Stuff just enough into a big plastic bag to make a giant ball to toss around. Just for fun, try putting them (temporarily) in some big space where no one expects to see them, like in the trunk of a friend's old car (surprise, surprise!).

Find the biggest and most colorful leaves to keep till the following autumn. Preserve them by soaking them in a solution of one part glycerin and two parts water; leave them soaking for several days, then dry them.

You can also put leaves between waxed paper, cover with a towel, then iron them (both sides) on an ironing board with a warm iron. This seals the waxed paper around the leaves, and you can trim off the excess paper.

44 No Time Like Snow Time

When it snows, build snow forts, snow caves, snow towers, snow tunnels, snow balls, snow cubes, snow bears, snow turtles, and of course, snow people.

Make snow angels (lie down in fresh snow and wave or flap your arms and legs to make the design). Fill the yard with them. Make them in rows—for a complete choir of snow angels.

While the snow's fresh and clean, make snow ice cream. Fill

a large bowl with snow and mix in a half cup of sugar, a cup of cream, two eggs, a teaspoon or so of vanilla, and a dash of salt. Taste it, adding more sugar or vanilla if necessary. Then stir in just enough milk (or cream or half-and-half) to get the desired consistency.

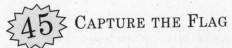 45 Capture the Flag

Join with friends and neighbors to play nighttime capture the flag.

Divide into teams. Go to a playground or park or other large, open area, and agree on a boundary that splits the territory in half between the two teams.

Each team has a flag—a scarf or bandana or rag. Place it in clear view in an open area near the back of each team's territory. The goal is to capture the other team's flag and bring it into their own territory.

Players crossing into the opposing team's territory can be captured simply by being tagged. They're kept in a holding area or jail, and can be released only by being tagged by one of their teammates (or by calling out "Jailbreak" when it's mutually agreed to by both teams).

46 > BRITISH BULLDOG

This game can get rough, so it isn't recommended for families with younger children unless you're very careful about not hurting them.

Join with friends and neighbors on this one; the more who play, the better.

Mark the playing area with two opposite boundaries. One person is the bulldog, and stands in the center area. The others line up behind one of the boundaries. When the bulldog gives the signal, the others have to run to safety behind the opposite boundary. But if the bulldog picks up someone completely off the ground and yells "One-two-three British bulldog!" before that person touches the ground again, he becomes a bulldog as well. Bulldogs can work together to pick up another player.

The last person caught becomes the bulldog for the next round.

47 > TUGGING WARS

Grab your friends and neighbors to join you for a tug of war. Mark two lines about fifteen feet apart. Lay a long rope (natural fiber is best) across them, perpendicular. At the very center of the rope, tie a rag.

Divide into two teams of evenly distributed weight and strength. Each team stands behind an opposing marked line. At the signal, they pull on the rope. The winner is the team that pulls the rag across its own line.

You can pretend that there's a raging fire, a deep rushing river, or a deep chasm in the space between the lines. Whichever team loses and gets dragged across its line will burn up, drown, or plummet to their deaths.

Add some variations: have everyone hold their right or left hand behind their back, have their ankles tied together, or blind-fold part of each team.

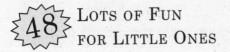 LOTS OF FUN
FOR LITTLE ONES

Let these suggestions stimulate further ideas for you:

- For very young children, don't forget those great back-yard games we all loved growing up, like duck duck goose, Simon says, hot potato, red light green light, hopscotch, and Mother may I.

- Have an afternoon backyard reading hour and invite the neighborhood children to join in. Read aloud your favorite picture books or storybooks.
- At night, play flashlight tag, combining tag with hide-and-seek. The person who's It tags another by shining her flashlight on them.
- Have everyone run backward all the way around the house.
- Make a volcano in a pile of sand or dirt. Build up a peak with a crater in it, and fill the crater with a mixture of baking soda and vinegar.

49 MORE IDEAS FOR THE LITTLE ONES

- Give each child an empty egg carton, and ask them to find or make something to go in each compartment.
- Put colored water (made with food coloring) in spray bottles, and let them paint pictures on the driveway. (It will easily wash off.) Or hang an old sheet from a clothesline or over a fence, and paint it with the spray bottles.

- While everyone joins in to wash the family car, also wash your bicycles, tricycles, toy wagons, and any other wheeled toys. As you do, splash one another with water and suds.
- Load up stuffed animals in a toy wagon, and take them for a ride around the neighborhood.
- Make a racetrack in the sandbox for toy trucks and cars.
- Decorate a shrub or small tree with a roll of toilet paper.

 ## More Outdoor Fun

Let these ideas stimulate even more for you:

- Camp out in the backyard. Set up a tent—or just sleep under the stars. Grill dinner and breakfast on the barbecue.
- Play imaginary sports with each other—throw and catch and kick imaginary balls.
- On the hottest days, turn on the lawn sprinklers and run through the spray. Or turn on a hose and play firefighters.
- Hide something on a tree limb and have everyone climb the tree to find it.

- For more rough-and-tumble times: play kick ball, dodge ball, or king of the mountain. Have a wrestling match or a race climbing up a tree.
- Make your own croquetlike game with an old tennis ball or golf ball, tin cans to shoot them through, and a hammer or baseball bat for a mallet.

SUMMARY

In this section you've read about twenty-two ways (and a few more) to entertain your family for free in your backyard. After trying them out, return to the ones that work best for your family, always revising them to make them your own.

3 Around Town

Wisdom shouts in the streets.
She cries out in the public square.

—PROVERBS 1:20

Doing only free things doesn't mean avoiding the avenues of commerce in your community.

In fact, you can frequent the stores and malls and marketplaces with fresher enjoyment and appreciation, free of the pressure to spend any money. You'll be better able to see those places—and the people there—for all that they are.

And if someone in one of these places tries to sell you something, explain what you're doing and get their take on it. Ask them what *they* do to entertain their family for free. You may get some fresh new ideas. (And they may even give you the scoop on some future bargains at their store that you can come back later and take advantage of.)

51 DAY ON THE TOWN

With sack lunches and water bottles in your backpack, head downtown for a day to remember. Choose a day when there are free special events at the library, museums, or elsewhere. (Or maybe there's a street fair or festival going on.) Take along your video camera (or borrow one to take), and record the day's experiences.

Start early, just as the first shops and businesses are opening. Browse in whatever stores you feel like exploring. Take note especially of the most friendly clerks and salespeople in the stores. (Have a premade certificate or thank-you card made up that you'll take back at the end of the day to "The Friendliest Store Clerk We Met Today.")

Choose a favorite spot to have your brown-bag lunch— perhaps a park or a quieter side street if you'd like a break— before once more plunging into the downtown crowds for the afternoon.

52 A NEW YOU

Try this at a discount clothing store, thriftshop, or any place with a good supply of used clothing—and dressing rooms.

From the available merchandise, have each person in your family put together the most outlandish outfit they can assemble and try it on. (Don't forget accessories.) Use your cell-phone camera to take a photo of each person in their outrageous finest. (Don't forget a group shot as well.) You can make a contest of it or just let everyone be a winner.

For variation or an extra challenge, have everyone (before you enter the store) choose a color that their outfit must include or feature. Or go for themes—say, '80s or Hawaiian or business chic or sportswear. Or too big or too tight. If the weather's hot outside, have everyone look for depths-of-winter apparel, or if it's wintertime, go for the best beach attire.

53 Imaginary Shopping Spree

Give each person an imaginary account with a specific dollar amount. Go into a department store and shop, making a mental or written list of everything you would purchase if you actually had the money.

Your objective could be for each person to pick out his own (or someone else's) birthday or Christmas gifts. Or to see how many separate items you can select and stay within your budget. Or to see what's the single *largest* item you could buy for the money.

You can take a photo with your cell-phone camera of every purchase you select. Or, once everyone has identified their items, go together around the store to see and comment on what each person chose.

Another approach would be to do this at home with the catalogs you've received from your favorite stores.

54 PECULIAR PICNICS

Here's a special way to eat out. Take a picnic lunch, plus a blanket or folding lawn chairs, and go out to some unusual place to have a family meal. Observe and discuss your surroundings and the people you see. Decide together on the most interesting thing you observe.

Some possible locations include a hospital lawn, a hotel lobby, an airport terminal or just outside the terminal (watch the planes landing and taking off), inside a train station, alongside a golf course, on a college campus, in front of a grocery store, hardware store, auto-parts store, paint store, pet shop, new- or used-car dealership, bookstore, furniture store, motor-cycle shop, barber or beauty salon, bank, electronics store, art gallery, police station, post office, or sporting goods store. The more unusual the picnic location, the better.

55 SCAVENGER FAMILY

Do a scavenger hunt (breaking into two teams or competing with another family).

One method is the bigger-and-better approach. Start with a small, relatively low-value item; go to a neighbor and ask to trade it for something either bigger or better. Do the same with this new item at another neighbor's house, then again and again. Set a time limit, with both teams meeting back at your home when time's up. Reward the team that returns with the biggest and best item.

Or simply make a long list of what kinds of items each team must scavenge from the neighborhood within the time limit. Some examples: something pink, something breakable, something to wear over your ears, something to keep in a junk drawer, something that glows in the dark, etc. The possibilities are endless—and endlessly fun.

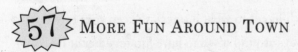 WATCH THEM WORK

Visit a construction site. From a safe distance, watch the workers and the machinery as they do what they do. Ask your child questions: What does that piece of equipment do? Why do you think those workers are doing that? What further work needs to be done here?

If you happen to catch the on-site foreman or overseer and can steal a moment of his time, mention that you're there just for the fun of watching and learning, and ask for a quick overview of what's happening there today. The overseer may even recommend the most interesting things to view and when and where to catch them if you can come back later. And he might even find a safe spot for getting an even closer look.

You could follow much the same approach at a retail store, a factory, or the office of a service provider.

57 MORE FUN AROUND TOWN

Let these stimulate further ideas:

- (Prepare for this one by having paper and pencils ready.) Take a fast walk together down an aisle in some store. Then have everyone write down as many different items as they can remember seeing on the shelves. Then walk back through to check your answers.

- Sit somewhere in a public place and people watch. Look at passersby and imagine what their lives are like—their first names, their homes, their neighborhoods, their occupations, their interests. Talk together about what others would guess about you in all these categories.

- Visit garage sales and yard sales, and look for giveaways. Use what you find to have a contest making sculptures or mobiles or some other creative object.

SUMMARY

In this section you've read of seven ways (and a few more) to entertain your family for free in your community. Every city and community is different in what it offers, so keep your eyes open to find more ways around town to have fun together at no cost.

4 Just Imagine

> Whatever is pure…lovely…admirable—if anything is
> excellent or praiseworthy—think about such things.
>
> —PHILIPPIANS 4:8

By far the most enriching and satisfying indoor entertainment is simply sharing together in stories. The activities in this section are largely about just that.

We interact with stories not just because we enjoy them but because we *need* them. As Robert McKee writes in *Story* (his highly acclaimed book on screenwriting), "Story isn't a flight from reality but a vehicle that carries us on our search for reality, our best effort to make sense out of the anarchy of existence."

Earlier McKee asks, "But what, after all, is entertainment? To be entertained is to be immersed in the ceremony of story to an intellectually and emotionally satisfying end."

Deep stuff, these stories—and so unbelievably fun, as we really get the hang of it!

58 ESTABLISHING A READ-ALOUD ROUTINE

A regular read-aloud time can become one of the most cherished experiences of childhood—taking our imaginations to new heights, while also revealing more about our own hearts and minds.

During read-aloud time, some children are content to sit and listen; many aren't. So, if your children aren't the type who easily sit and listen, try these basic rules:

1. While listening, you can pursue any other activity (drawing, playing with a toy, building something, etc.) as long as it's quiet and not distracting.

2. Only the reader speaks; save your questions and comments for afterward.

To test the kinds of read-aloud books your family enjoys most, check out several possible items from your local library. Here's a wide-ranging set of classic books to consider:

All-of-a-Kind Family by Sydney Taylor

Billy and Blaze by C. W. Anderson

Mary Poppins by P. L. Travers

The Napping House by Audrey Wood and Don Wood

59 YOUR FAVORITE CHILDHOOD BOOKS

The most universal and timelessly appealing form of entertainment is storytelling. As your family grows in storytelling and read-aloud skills, you're able to tap into endless entertainment treasures, thanks to the unrivaled abundance of quality children's literature and youth literature. Moreover, because listening to stories (as well as reading them) is ultimately far more effective than any electronic media in developing a child's imagination and intelligence, your children will grow to find written and spoken stories to be incomparably satisfying.

Be committed to storytelling and reading aloud. To start, simply read aloud to your children your favorite childhood books.

Do you consider yourself a poor reader? Practice will only improve your skills. So relax…and read!

(Several recommendations for good read-aloud books will continue on the coming pages.)

60 ENTERING PICTURE-BOOK PARADISE

For your best picture books to enjoy together, the list below represents just a few of the beginner favorites for families everywhere. Find them in your local library:

*Alexander and the Terrible, Horrible, No Good, Very Bad
Day* by Judith Viorst

anything by Beatrix Potter (such as *The Tales of Peter Rabbit*)

Caps for Sale by Esphyr Slobodkina

The Cat in the Hat by Dr. Seuss

Corduroy by Don Freeman

Goodnight Moon and *The Runaway Bunny* by Margaret
Wise Brown

The Little Engine That Could by Watty Piper

The Little House by Virginia Lee Burton

Make Way for Ducklings and *Blueberries for Sal* by Robert
McCloskey

Mike Mulligan and His Steam Shovel by Virginia Lee Burton

One Fine Day by Nonny Hogrogian

Ox-Cart Man by Donald Hall

The Story About Ping by Marjorie Flack

The Very Hungry Caterpillar by Eric Carle

 ## WIDER HORIZONS IN PICTURE BOOKS

The illustrated books recommended below are a bit more involved than the simpler picture books of the very early preschool
years, though they still hold magic for very young hearts.

Some favorite series of illustrated books include:

the Alfie series by Shirley Hughes

the Amelia Bedelia books by Peggy Parish and Herman
     Parish

the Babar books by Jean de Brunhoff

the Curious George books by H. A. Rey and Margret Rey

the Frog and Toad series by Arnold Lobel

the Madeline series by Ludwig Bemelmans

books by Richard Scarry

Other favorite books include:

Aesop's fables

Alice in Wonderland and *Through the Looking-Glass* by Lewis
     Carroll

the fairy tales of Hans Christian Andersen and the brothers
     Grimm

the Uncle Remus stories by Joel Chandler Harris

Winnie-the-Pooh and *The House at Pooh Corner* by A. A.
     Milne

 CLASSIC READ-ALOUD CHAPTER BOOKS

The chapter endings in these books for children usually con-
clude in a way that leaves your kids begging to start another

chapter. But half the fun is having to wait till another nightly story time to see what happens next.

Particularly enjoyable chapter-book series include *The Chronicles of Narnia* by C. S. Lewis and the Little House books (including *Little House on the Prairie*) by Laura Ingalls Wilder. A few other classic favorites include:

Adam of the Road by Elizabeth Janet Gray

Amos Fortune, Free Man by Elizabeth Yates

The Bronze Bow and *The Sign of the Beaver* by Elizabeth George Speare

Charlotte's Web, Stuart Little, and *The Trumpet of the Swan* by E. B. White

The Cricket in Times Square by George Selden

The Door in the Wall by Marguerite de Angeli

King of the Wind by Marguerite Henry

The Trumpeter of Krakow by Eric P. Kelly

The Wind in the Willows by Kenneth Grahame

63 RHYME TIME

Try starting your read-aloud time with a poem. Some classic collections of poetry for children include:

A Child's Garden of Verses by Robert Louis Stevenson

Mother Goose nursery rhymes

Sing-Song by Christina Rossetti

When We Were Very Young and *Now We Are Six* by A. A.
    Milne (the Winnie-the-Pooh author)

You can also search (online or at the library) for these examples of classic read-aloud poems:

"Answer to a Child's Question" by Samuel Taylor
    Coleridge

"Be Strong" by M. D. Babcock

"The Children's Hour" by Henry Wadsworth
    Longfellow

"The Duel" and "Wynken, Blynken, and Nod" by
    Eugene Field

"Eletelephony" by Laura Richards

"Home" by Edgar A. Guest

"If" by Rudyard Kipling

"Jabberwocky" by Lewis Carroll

"Little Lamb" by William Blake

"Nonsenses" and "An Alphabet" by Edward Lear

"The Spider and the Fly" by Mary Howitt

"Stopping by Woods on a Snowy Evening" by Robert
    Frost

"Trees" by Joyce Kilmer

64 READING ALOUD AS YOUR KIDS GROW OLDER

As your children move into their later elementary school years and middle school years, the following favorite classics can help hold their attention in read-aloud time:

The Adventures of Huckleberry Finn by Mark Twain

Anne of Green Gables by L. M. Montgomery

The Call of the Wild by Jack London

The Dark Frigate by Charles Boardman Hawes

The Hobbit and *The Lord of the Rings* by J. R. R. Tolkien

Kidnapped, Treasure Island, and *The Black Arrow* by
    Robert Louis Stevenson

The Little Prince by Antoine de Saint-Exupéry

The Merry Adventures of Robin Hood by Howard Pyle

The Ox-Bow Incident by Walter Van Tilburg Clark

Robinson Crusoe by Daniel Defoe

The Silver Sword by Ian Serraillier

Sir Gibbie by George MacDonald

The Swiss Family Robinson by J. D. Wyss

To Kill a Mockingbird by Harper Lee

The Wonderful Wizard of Oz by L. Frank Baum

The Yearling by Marjorie Kinnan Rawlings

65 SHORT STORIES—LONG ON ENJOYMENT

Short stories are meant to be read in a single setting, and a read-aloud setting at home is the best. Find these classics at your local library (they're often included in anthologies):

"Butch Minds the Baby" by Damon Runyon

"The Celebrated Jumping Frog of Calaveras County" by Mark Twain

"A Child's Dream of a Star" by Charles Dickens

"The Devoted Friend" by Oscar Wilde

"The Enchanted Bluff" by Willa Cather

"The Golden Key" by George MacDonald

"How the Camel Got His Hump" by Rudyard Kipling

"Quality" by John Galsworthy

"The Ransom of Red Chief" and "The Cop and the Anthem" by O. Henry

"Something Lost" by Jack Schaefer

"Three Questions" and "How Much Land Does a Man Need?" by Leo Tolstoy

"To Build a Fire" and "Love of Life" by Jack London

"Two Soldiers" by William Faulkner

66 Are You Spooked Yet?

When everyone's feeling safe and secure, have a night of read-aloud ghost stories and mystery stories (if your children aren't too young for them). Include your own made-up ghost stories as well.

For read-aloud mysteries, choose one of Arthur Conan Doyle's Sherlock Holmes stories.

For ghost stories and horror stories, consider something by Edgar Allan Poe, such as "The Black Cat," "The Cask of Amontillado," "The Gold Bug," "The Masque of the Red Death," "The Tell-Tale Heart," or "William Wilson."

Or try any of these classics:

"August Heat" and "The Beast with Five Fingers" by
    W. F. Harvey

"The Furnished Room" by O. Henry

"The Ghost Ship" by Richard B. Middleton

"The Horla" by Guy de Maupassant

"Markheim" by Robert Louis Stevenson

"An Occurrence at Owl Creek Bridge" by Ambrose Bierce

"They" and "The Phantom Rickshaw" by Rudyard
    Kipling

67 Morning Grooming Skit

On a family skit night, try this favorite.

One person stands behind a table, facing forward with his hands securely behind his back. The other stands behind him, head bowed, and places her arms under and out through his. Her arms now serve as his.

On the table are a toothbrush and toothpaste, shaving cream and razor (bladeless), and hair gel and hairbrush. The first person now goes through his morning routine to look his best—cleaning his teeth, shaving, and grooming his hair. But it's the second person's hands that will do all the work—as best she can, though she can't see what's on the table.

The first person narrates each procedure to cue the other person on what to do: "I get up in the morning, and the first thing I do is brush my teeth…"

68 Shopping Skit

For family skit night, here's a test of everyone's physical coordination.

With everyone standing, one person narrates a shopping

trip, detail by detail, and demonstrates motions for everything she describes. Everyone follows her example—and they keep doing each motion while slowly adding on others.

Narrator: "I went to a department store, I got on the elevator, and I rode up and down, up and down." (Motion: keep bending knees.)

"I bought a sewing machine, and I treadled and I treadled." (Tap one foot.)

"I bought a pair of scissors—I snipped and snipped." (Clipping motion with right fingers.)

"I bought a bongo, and I drummed and drummed." (Beating motion with the left palm.)

"I bought new glasses, and I looked and looked everywhere." (Rotate head side to side and all around.)

Can everyone do them all at once?

69 A WORLD TO PLAY IN

In playtime, step into a faraway place or the long-ago past. Pretend to be Vikings, Huns, samurai, pirates, knights and ladies, wilderness trailblazers, western pioneers, lunar astronauts, Civil War soldiers, Roman legionnaires, Arab merchants, arctic explorers, jungle explorers, Native American buffalo hunters, Greek orators and Olympians, Polynesian seafarers, pioneer aviators, a Chinese emperor's court…or whoever your children are most interested in at the time.

Set the tone and flavor by reading aloud some stories about your chosen era or group. If you want costumes, use whatever's on hand plus lots of imagination. Fashion items like tools, shields, and armor from cardboard.

Then let it unfold. Articulate quests and challenges: rescue the captives, climb the peak, repel the invaders, reach the shore, sway the masses, find the treasure, build the fortress, achieve the dream.

70 BRING IN THE CUSTOMERS

Imagine owning your own retail shop in some line of business that you find enjoyable, and make advertisements to bring in customers. You could all work together in the same imaginary establishment, or let each person envision his own (the crazier and more creative, the better).

Use colored markers or crayons on blank paper, plus art from magazines, to create your ads for posters, billboards, magazines, newspapers, and the Internet. Use a cell-phone video camera to record television commercials (both ad spots and infomercials). Think about how your own Web site should look, on paper at least.

Come up with slogans, jingles, brand names—the works. Decide which celebrities will want to endorse your store and write out their endorsements.

Put together a flyer listing your assorted products and their many features. Make a big splash especially for your biggest-selling product.

 ## CHAIN STORY

One of you starts telling a made-up story but goes only partway before letting the next person tell more of it, and then the next person, and so on. This can continue on and on, and there are many variations.

At the pass-along point, the person telling the story can point to or mention an object in the room, and the person continuing the story then has to incorporate that object into the story in a logical way.

Or you can simply stop in midsentence. "He ran to the edge

of the cliff, where he—" and that's the point where the next storyteller picks it up.

For a longer activity, you can do this in writing. Each person fills a page (or half page or quarter page), then passes the notebook to the next person to continue.

72 DREAM HOUSE

Plan your family's dream house. (Pretend it's all being provided to you at no cost—and plan accordingly.) It can be a castle, a mansion on a country estate, a skyscraping penthouse in an urban hot-spot, or the most practical and reasonable place in all of suburbia. Let it be whatever you want—and talk together about why you'd want it that way.

On blank paper (graph paper if you have it), sketch out a floor plan in pencil. Draw in every kind of space you want it to have, for every function.

Give thought to what kind of materials you want, in every part and detail, and list those beside the floor plan. Think about windows, flooring, walls, ceilings.

Plan the exterior and the grounds as well. What do you want it all to look and feel like?

73 DREAM VACATION

Plan your most delightful family vacation—one of those once-in-a-lifetime getaways. (Pretend it's all being provided at no cost to you—and plan accordingly.) Expect to be gone for a month or three or six or a whole year.

Get out an atlas and take note of all the places you've always wanted to see, the ideal locations for all you've wanted to experience and do. Talk together about why you've wanted to see and do these things.

Schedule the entire trip, day by day and week by week—where you'll stay, what you'll do there, and what you'll want to see. Go online to search for lodging as well as other kinds of tourist information. Decide on the most enjoyable modes of travel between all your stops.

74 HOMEMADE COMIC BOOKS

Create your own comic books. They can be funny cartoons or centered around action, adventure, danger, or romance.

You may want to pencil out a rough draft first, using an

ordinary notebook, and wait to make the final product until you're pretty sure what you want it to look like.

When you're ready to make the final version, use a ruler to mark the straight lines for the panels. Do the drawings first in pencil, erasing and refining as you go. Then go over the pencil lines (and the words) in black ink. Finally add in color with crayons or colored markers.

Spend some time getting the cover and title just right.

If you really enjoy this endeavor, plan for a series of comic books with the same characters.

75 Mars or Bust

Congratulations! Your family's been chosen to join a new human colony on Mars!

Food, clothing, and toiletries will all be provided, plus plenty of living space. You can take along personal items—but no more for each of you than can normally fill a small rental trailer (eight by five by five feet, or two hundred cubic feet). What will each of you choose to have with you on Mars? Make your list.

Whoops! Looks like the spacecraft's overloaded. Now each person can take only enough to fit in a travel trunk (three by two by two feet, or twelve cubic feet). Revise your list.

Whoops! A new calculation. All your stuff must fit in a small carry-on (twenty-two by eighteen by ten inches—less than two and a half cubic feet). Now, what will you take?

76 MUSIC TO YOUR EARS

Write your own song—music and lyrics. In fact, write several. Put together an original musical play, opera, or concert set.

Even if no one in your family plays an instrument, you can still sing your new creation with your voices.

For more music fun:

- Play name that song. Have someone clap the rhythm to a song while the others try to guess what it is. If that's too hard, whistle or hum the first few notes.

- Make your home a concert hall by taking turns having each person play a prearranged set of their favorite recorded music. Introduce each selection by identifying the composer and the artist (and their backgrounds, if you know them). Include a short description of why you like it—or write those things down in a handwritten program to give everyone.

77 TIME-WARP DRAMA

Have a family skit or drama night where you imagine what it would be like for different characters from different eras or locations to meet one another. (Or just talk about what these encounters would be like.)

Some suggestions:

Adolf Hitler meets Helen Keller

The Beatles meet Shakespeare

Abraham Lincoln meets Saddam Hussein

Elvis Presley meets Beethoven

King Arthur meets Mickey Mouse

Princess Diana meets Guinevere

Albert Einstein meets Tom Sawyer

Muhammad Ali meets Joan of Arc

Benedict Arnold meets Pinocchio

Julius Caesar meets Thomas Jefferson

Christopher Columbus meets Geronimo

Mother Teresa meets Attila the Hun

Robin Hood meets Cleopatra

Charles Dickens meets Alexander the Great

Queen Victoria meets Al Capone

Babe Ruth meets Napoleon

Mahatma Gandhi meets Marie Antoinette

Benjamin Franklin meets Bill Cosby

Rembrandt meets Mark Twain

Theodore Roosevelt meets Michael Jackson

 ## 78 More Fun with Your Imaginations

Let these ideas stir up others of your own:

- Imagine that each of you is given a time machine, but it can be used only once. To what location and time period would each of you want to go?

- Talk together about the celebrity you would most like to meet. If you could spend a day with that person, what would you do together? If that person came to your house to spend the day, what would you plan to do?

- What new invention would you most like to create? What problem would it solve, or what would it accomplish?

- What historical figure would you most like to interview? What are the top three questions you would like to ask that person?

- Describe your ideal job. What kind of work do you think would be absolutely the most fulfilling for you?

SUMMARY

In this section you've seen twenty-one ways (and more) to entertain your family for free simply by putting your imaginations to work. This is the key to the best kinds of entertainment. Keep stretching your imaginations to constantly find new ways for having fun together.

5 Out in Nature

O LORD, your unfailing love fills the earth.

—PSALM 119:64

All of nature is an arena where your family belongs. The big story of who you essentially are as a family cannot be adequately learned and retold without seeing yourselves in the context of God's beautiful earth and the vastness of his universe.

Most of us don't live very close to nature anymore; when we want to get closer, sometimes it isn't cheap to do so. Mountain forests, wilderness valleys, serene deserts, unplowed plains, undisturbed beaches—they're probably some distance from your house. But in whatever way and to whatever degree you as a family can sample this world in its rawest freshness, the more you'll discover about yourselves.

79 > FOREST WONDERS

Try these while hiking in the woods:

Look for the tallest tree, the tree with the widest trunk, the crookedest tree, the tree with the prettiest shape, the best climbing tree (and take time to climb it!), the tree with the prettiest leaves or needles, the tree where you'd most like to put a tree house and live in it.

Stop and play hide-and-seek along the way. Climb rock formations you pass. Look for fish in the streams.

Look for and identify types of trees, insects, wildflowers, birds, and reptiles. Find the best-looking rocks and pebbles.

Pick a visible landmark ahead and have everyone guess how many steps it will take you to get there. Then count them as you walk at a normal pace.

Sing aloud "The Happy Wanderer" and teach it to everyone else.

Get perfectly still and absolutely quiet. What do you hear?

80 > STAR STARING

Get away from the city lights to where you can get a better look at the stars; the best time is when there's no moon and the stars are more visible. Think and talk together about how small they look compared to how vastly tremendous in size they really are. Think and talk together about how great the distance is between them and us. Recall that the Bible says that God created them and calls them all by name.

Let your eyes get used to the darkness. Then find major constellations—especially Orion, the Big and Little Dippers, and Cassiopeia—and teach their names to your children. Show them how to find the North Star (Polaris) using the outside edge of the Big Dipper to point the way. Observe any planets that are visible.

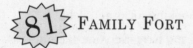 Family Fort

Build a fortress together in the woods. This will probably be a long-term project, so find a place that's remote.

Start where there's a large rock formation or a huge downed tree. Build upward and outward from there. Use downed branches, logs, and rocks of all sizes to build walls and ledges, ramparts and bastions, casements and turrets. Daub holes with mud mixed with grass or sticks or straw or leaves or pine needles.

Dig bunkers and tunnels. Carve out trenches and moats, and pile up berms beside them.

Fashion storehouses and barracks. Lash branches together to make stockades, ladders, towers, parapets, and banner poles. Use rocks to form firepits and fire rings. Use larger rocks or stumps for furniture.

Give it a strong name; use your family's name plus words like *citadel* or *fortress*.

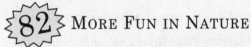 MORE FUN IN NATURE

Let these ideas stimulate even more for you:

- Plan a weekend series of favorite hikes and take turns choosing the location.
- On a trip to the woods, bring along pocketknives. Find some sticks and practice whittling and carving.
- Hunt for lizards, butterflies, bugs, and frogs.
- Try bird-watching (spring and fall are often the best times). Take binoculars to a park or another wooded area and start observing. Take notes of what you see and hear. Take along a guide to birds that you've checked out from the library.
- Dig up worms for bait and go fishing.

- Take paper bags with you on a nature walk to collect interesting leaves, acorns, rocks, etc.
- Take a notebook with you as you hike. Describe and map the terrain (like Lewis and Clark).

SUMMARY

In this brief section you've seen several ways to entertain your family for free out in nature. Search far and wide to find the most accessible and stimulating places for your family to explore and enjoy the great outdoors.

6 Rituals and Routines

Laughter and bread go together.

—ECCLESIATES 10:19

This section features one activity that can serve as a lasting link to everything else in this book—the keeping of a family diary or journal. (See number 83 below.)

With a few disciplines here, a few habits there, a few new traditions and patterns…you can easily build into your family's mindset a healthy approach to entertainment that's perpetually reinforcing.

Use the ideas here to spur you on to discovering just-right rituals and routines for your family's most memorable pleasures.

83 DAILY MEMORIES

Together, keep a family diary or family journal where you record a few of each day's most memorable events.

Do this around the dinner table after the evening meal. As an added highlight, flip back to previous pages in the journal to read (and re-enjoy!) what happened a month ago today or a year ago today or two years ago.

To get the most value, it's more important to be regular about this than it is to record lengthy entries. Jot down just the highlights. In the months and years to come, as you review what you've written, memories will be triggered and you'll all want to reminisce. As a family, your identity and sense of history and destiny will deepen a little every day.

If you miss a day or two, don't worry; just catch up with a few summary lines.

84 EACH ONE'S SPECIAL DAY

Designate a different day of the week as each child's recurring special day.

On their special day, they get to choose part or all of the breakfast menu (maybe lunch and dinner too) and perhaps even be excused from certain chores. They can also choose which book or books to read from during that evening's read-aloud story time.

Other potential special day privileges:

- the choicest seat when riding in the family vehicle
- going first when games are played
- the first servings at mealtime
- permission to climb in bed with parents
- a date with one or more parents
- candy or another favorite treat
- having a friend over for the evening or overnight
- choosing a favorite movie to watch or music to listen to
- sleeping in the guest bedroom or another special place
- a one-on-one phone conversation with a favorite relative
- any activity or experience each child values most

85 FIRSTS

Each winter, on the day of the first snowfall, read aloud together the picture book *The Snowy Day* by Ezra Jack Keats, *The Big Snow* by Berta Hader and Elmer Hader, or Hans Christian Andersen's classic fairy tale *The Snow Queen* (the full text is available online at several Web sites). Also check out from the library the 1982 wordless animated movie *The Snowman,* which is based on the children's book by Raymond Briggs.

Each spring, on the first day you see a robin land in your yard, have a picnic. If it's too cold to do it outside, spread a blanket on the family-room floor and do it there.

Each autumn, when you first see a V-formation of geese flying south or the first morning frost, drink hot apple cider and read aloud the poem "When the Frost Is on the Punkin" by James Whitcomb Riley.

86 HALFWAY BIRTHDAY

Have a surprise party by celebrating a family member's birthday six months early. Give gag gifts that are half missing—like one old shoe or one glove or one sock or one earring. Offer the gifts in boxes only half covered in wrapping paper and ribbon. Fashion birthday cards, then cut and throw away half of each one. Make a birthday cake, but cut away half of it before serving it. Use plastic forks with half the tines clipped off. Serve drinks in half-filled glasses. Sing the "Happy Birthday" song only halfway through. Play pin the tail with a big drawing of only half a donkey.

Afterward, promise the honoree that you'll all celebrate again—and more completely—on the actual birthday date.

87 Mix It Up at Mealtime

Make mealtime more fun with occasional changes such as:

- Cook breakfast outside on the barbecue grill. (Breakfast burgers, anyone?) That night, serve waffles or scrambled eggs for dinner.

- Serve a formal dinner for just the family, with each person taking turns being the waiter and everyone learning proper etiquette. For extra fun, make the menu unelegant: hot dogs, macaroni and cheese, and Jell-O. Keep everything else first-class formal. (Macaroni and cheese by candlelight!)

- Have a meal in an unusual place: the garage, the front sidewalk, the garden. Or pack it up and eat in the car as you drive around with no particular destination.

- Eat a multicourse meal in reverse, dessert first. Serve soup on a plate, salad in a drinking glass, and water in a bowl.

88 Pass-along Trophy

When you play your family's favorite card game or board game, have a pass-along trophy that's awarded to the winner.

An everyday usable item works especially well—like a favorite plate or glass. It should, of course, be something different from your everyday dishware or drinkware. If you don't have one that's unique, you can often find something at the freebies table at a thrift store. The more cool it is, the better—like an engraved pewter platter or an embellished German-style beer stein with a lid and thumb lever.

The privilege of using the trophy continues until someone else wins a later round of your favorite game.

If you have two or three favorite games, designate trophies for each. Or you can award the trophy for whatever game you play each time you have a family game night.

SUMMARY

In this section you've seen six ways of establishing some entertaining traditions in your family. Keep exploring new ones that work best for your family.

7 Holidays

This is the day that the LORD has made;

let us rejoice and be glad in it.

—PSALM 118:24

Holidays were mostly made for entertainment—feasting, music, and congregating to remember again our oldest and deepest stories.

Help your family enter into all that with relish. Help them see each holiday not as a day off—a day to do nothing—but as a day to pack with meaning and pleasure.

Avoid as well the extreme of packing holidays with what has to be purchased. If holidays drain your funds more than they fill your soul, something's wrong.

89 Cookie Artistry

Bake homemade cookies (using your favorite recipe), then have everyone join in to decorate them for the holiday or occasion. Before eating them, display them and invite friends and relatives over. (Or, for even more fun, have your guests join in the decorating.)

Cut out shapes freehand if you don't have holiday cookie cutters.

Use food coloring in homemade frosting to get a variety of colors. Use whatever's on hand for toppings. Chop up nuts and raisins and other dried fruits. Make chocolate sprinkles by running chocolate kisses or chocolate bars through a garlic press or food chopper. Or turn a chocolate bar into shavings with a potato peeler.

Make colored sugar sprinkles by adding a few drops of food coloring to white sugar, then shake in a closed container. Add more drops to get a more intense color.

90 No-Budget Valentine's Day

Make your own Valentine's Day cards to give to each other and to friends. Try making your own pop-ups inside the cards, with hearts and flowers that spring up (from glued-on paper stems) when the card is opened.

Get the whole family involved in planning and preparing a special evening meal honoring Mom and Dad and their loving marriage. Choose the menu from whatever's in the pantry and the fridge. Do it up right with candlelight. Draw and cut out paper flowers for a romantic bouquet.

Another decorating idea is to make a wreath from cutout hearts colored red and pink, and hang it on the wall. Or use giant hearts for placemats.

After dinner, let Mom and Dad tell the story of how they met and married. Let the kids ask questions, if they want, and have them talk about the kind of person they hope to marry someday.

91 ENJOYING EASTER

Besides munching candy from Easter baskets and hunting colored eggs, sample the Bible's account of the death and resurrection of Jesus Christ (which is why Easter is celebrated) by reading aloud from Luke 23–24 (or John 19–20 or Matthew 27–28) and Paul's sermon on the resurrection in 1 Corinthians 15.

Other read-aloud selections appropriate for this holiday include *The Tale of Three Trees* by Angela Elwell Hunt and *The Story of Easter* by Christopher Doyle. Older children might enjoy the short story–play "Today Is Friday" by Ernest Hemingway and the poem "Death Be Not Proud" by John Donne.

For preschoolers, consider reading the Easter story as it's written in your favorite children's story Bible (*The Beginners Bible, The First Step Bible,* or *The Praise Bible*).

 CELEBRATE INDEPENDENCE

For the Fourth of July, bake a birthday cake to celebrate America's Independence Day and put fifty candles on it (if you have that many on hand)—one for each state. Decorate it in red, white, and blue.

Choose from these patriotic classics in your family's read-aloud time: the chapter books *Johnny Tremain* by Esther Forbes and *Guns for General Washington* by Seymour Reit; the stories "The Man Without a Country" by Edward Everett Hale, "The Little Lord of the Manor" by Elbridge S. Brooks, "Old Esther Dudley" by Nathaniel Hawthorne, and "The Spy" by James Fenimore Cooper; and the poems "Paul Revere's Ride" by Henry

Wadsworth Longfellow, "America" by Samuel Smith, "America the Beautiful" by Katherine Lee Bates, "Barbara Frietchie" by John Greenleaf Whittier, and "Once to Every Man and Nation" (from "The Present Crisis") by James Russell Lowell.

93 ⊰ MORE HOLIDAY READING

Plan for special family read-aloud times on national occasions and holidays. The read-aloud selections below can be found online at various Web sites or in resources at your local library.

- Martin Luther King Jr. Day (third Monday in January): Dr. King's "I have a dream" speech given on August 28, 1963, in Washington, D.C.

- Abraham Lincoln's birthday (February 12): Lincoln's Gettysburg Address and his second inaugural address

- George Washington's birthday (February 22): Washington's Farewell Address

- Memorial Day (last Monday in May): the poem "Heroes" by William Canton

- Labor Day (first Monday in September): Henry Wadsworth Longfellow's poem "The Village Blacksmith"

- Columbus Day (October 12): Edgar Guest's poem "The Things That Haven't Been Done Before," and the poem "Columbus" ("Sail On! Sail On!") by Cincinnatus Hiner Miller (Joaquin Miller)
- Veterans Day (November 11): the poem "In Flanders Field" by John McCrae

 GIVING THANKS

At Thanksgiving, read aloud Robert Louis Stevenson's brief poem "A Prayer of Thanksgiving." Remember what this day is really all about—why it has been set aside as a holiday. Spend a few moments praying together as a family, expressing your gratitude to God for your specific blessings.

Before you pray, take some relaxed, informal time (perhaps after the big meal) to identify what you as a family have to be truly thankful for. You may want to write these things down. In the future, you can make it a Thanksgiving tradition to review your list from the previous year. Think about your relationships and friendships, your life and health, and all the various ways in which your needs have been met. Thank God especially for the people and events he has used in your life to make you more aware of him.

95 A CHRISTMAS TREE TRULY YOUR OWN

Plan ahead to decorate your Christmas tree with only home-made decorations.

Glue Popsicle sticks together to fashion simple stars and snowflakes for ornaments, then glue and glitter them so they sparkle. Tie on colorful yarn or string to use to hang them.

Make picture ornaments by cutting out scenes from old Christmas cards. Punch holes around the outside, then thread yarn through the holes to make a colorful border. Do the same with pictures you draw of the people and images in the Christmas story—baby Jesus, Mary, Joseph, shepherds, wisemen, cattle, donkeys, sheep, camels, and the star.

String popcorn on thread for popcorn garlands. This task can seem tedious, so pop enough corn for everyone to eat along the way, and put in a favorite Christmas movie to watch while you're doing it.

96 CHRISTMAS FILM FESTIVAL

Talk about (and watch) your favorite Christmas movies (check them out from the library).

After watching them, have an Oscar night to decide together your choices in these categories:

- Best Christmas Movie
- Best Actor in a Christmas Movie
- Best Actress in a Christmas Movie
- Best Supporting Actor in a Christmas Movie
- Best Supporting Actress in a Christmas Movie
- Best Director of a Christmas Movie
- Best Costumes in a Christmas Movie
- Best Song in a Christmas Movie
- Best Christmas Comedy
- Best Adaptation of Charles Dickens's *A Christmas Carol*
- Best Movie that Captures the Real Meaning of Christmas

Bring out plenty of popcorn to snack on while watching the movies, as well as pickles, carrot sticks, apple slices, and other favorite crunchable movie snacks. Finish with Christmas cookies and eggnog or hot chocolate.

 97 CHRISTMASTIME READ-ALOUD

At Christmastime, gather around the tree and read aloud from these proven children's books:

The Best Christmas Pageant Ever by Barbara Robinson

A Christmas Carol by Charles Dickens

Christmas in the Big Woods by Laura Ingalls Wilder

The Crippled Lamb by Max Lucado

How the Grinch Stole Christmas! by Dr. Seuss

The Polar Express by Chris Van Allsburg

Include some classic short stories, such as:

"The Gift of the Magi" by O. Henry

"The Gifts of the Child Christ" and "A Scot's Christmas Story" by George MacDonald

"The Little Match Girl" by Hans Christian Andersen.

"The Nutcracker and the Mouse King" by E. T. A. Hoffmann

"Where Love Is, God Is" by Leo Tolstoy

And enjoy these classic poems:

"Christmas Bells" and "The Three Kings" by Henry Wadsworth Longfellow

"Christmas Everywhere" by Phillips Brooks

"The Night Before Christmas" by Clement Clarke Moore

 MEMORABLE CHRISTMAS

More fun ideas for this Christmas:

- Go caroling in costume as characters from Charles Dickens's *A Christmas Carol*—or like biblical characters from the Nativity account in the Gospels (Matthew 1–2 and Luke 2).

- Cut out snowflakes from folded white coffee filters. Hang them with string from the ceiling or on the Christmas tree.
- Pull out the sleeping bags and spend a night sleeping around the Christmas tree. Leave the tree lights on all night.
- Decide together on your favorite Christmas songs and your favorite recorded Christmas music. Set aside a night to listen to your favorites and talk about why you like them.
- Construct a homemade Nativity scene with cutout paper figures.
- Together, thank God for his good news contained in the Bible of our salvation through Jesus Christ.

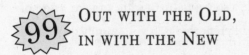

99 OUT WITH THE OLD, IN WITH THE NEW

For New Year's Day, have the traditional black-eyed peas for dinner (or substitute any kind of beans or peas you have on hand).

Talk together about your biggest goals and dreams for the

coming year. What are you most excited about and eager for? What are you most anxious about? What are you most confident about? (Read together Robert Frost's poem "The Road Not Taken.")

Also relive your best memories of the preceding year. What were the most fun occasions? the biggest challenges? the most valuable lessons?

Take time to pray together as a family and ask God to guide and protect you in the coming year. Express also to him your gratitude for all that he brought into your life in the previous year and how these things have made you all better persons— and together, a better family.

SUMMARY

Here you've been given eleven ways (and more) of entertaining your family for free at holiday times. Keep establishing these enjoyable traditions, while also being free and flexible to let go of them and try new and different things as your family grows and changes.

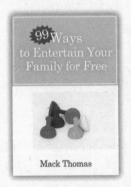